THE NOIR AMERICAN

26/4/19

To John
a pleasure to read
with you
Tony

THE NOIR AMERICAN

AND OTHER POEMS

Tony Roberts

TONY ROBERTS

Shoestring Press

Printed by imprintdigital
Upton Pyne, Exeter
www.digital.imprint.co.uk

Typesetting and cover design by narrator
www.narrator.me.uk
info@narrator.me.uk
033 022 300 39

Published by Shoestring Press
19 Devonshire Avenue, Beeston, Nottingham, NG9 1BS
(0115) 925 1827
www.shoestringpress.co.uk

First published 2018
© Copyright: Tony Roberts
© Copyright cover image: George Goode

The moral right of the author has been asserted.

ISBN 978-1-912524-15-0

ACKNOWLEDGEMENTS

Acknowledgements are due to the editors of the following journals and books in whose pages some of these poems first appeared:

Agenda, Areté, Critical Survey, Great River Review, London Magazine, Magma, New Walk Magazine, PN Review, Poetry London, Poetry Review, Stand.

Accompanied Voices, edited by John Greening (The Boydell Press, 2015)
Strike up the Band: Poems for John Lucas at 80, edited by Merryn Williams (Plas Gwyn Books, 2017)
Outsiders, Tony Roberts (Shoestring Press, 2010)
Drawndark, Tony Roberts (Shoestring Press, 2014)

And thanks to George Goode for his thoughts on the poems.

To Chris, Kate & Joe, Dan, Jen & Theo

CONTENTS

The Noir American

PROLOGUE: LE NOIR AMÉRICAIN

They've come from her place, where they broke the bed.
Experience has taught him jazzmen
save their worst timing for chicks. A drag
but *tant pis* as they say here: that's too bad.
He'll drown his conscience after the last set.
For now he needs to get it off his chest.
If ripeness is all then he's a *pamplemousse*.
Sabine's hip; she'll sense that something's in the air
aside from smoke and booze—his oxygen.
He splays long fingers on the table top.
Each knuckle is a point he wants to make.
Behind them Madeleine uncouples stools.

He tells her Pres once fired a drummer—
the cat just couldn't keep his fat mouth shut.
One night he filled a silence asking Pres
when the two of them last played together.
Pres fixed him with that wasted look and said
'Tonight.' He tells her to be pretty,
blonde and twenty, to have the tiniest
high rent apartment on the Left Bank
and the nicest ass, to be hanging out
with him, a black jazzman, a felon, drunk,
is to have this world sincerely by the balls.
Sure he loves her. But Paris is Disneyland.

Granted, here the two of them can sashay
arm in arm along the Champs Elysées
and for a quarter dine on onion soup
and *pâté de maison*, with that great bread.
Here it's not about his colour, just his sax.
And color blindness is the greatest thing—

except one time a color-blind white boy
told him that his skin looked 'kinda green.'
He twirls his empty glass for Madeleine.
See color's just another fucked up way
of seeing things. One hand begins to phrase.

He's sorted, thanks to her. But in New York
smart cats are soaking up the kind of sound
that's not been spilt in Europe yet. He's cut
off from his lab. The stuff that Trane and Monk
are into—and then Miles, the modal thing—
back home that's going down and he's not there.
Besides, they don't know shake from burger here.
Who's heard of Jackie Robinson? He nods,
sniffs at the flocked wallpaper, the drapes,
the tight-ass stage space—gestures at her glass
(Maybe he'll start the set with 'Lover Man').
She covers her *vin rouge*, her nails bright black.

He takes her fingers in his hand. You start
to doubt your honesty, then everyone's.
You dig? She stares. You ask yourself if all
this adulation is just kissing ass,
cats chasing bucks, or trying to be hip.
Anti-bourgeois, he pronounces carefully.
And here in France you clap the bum notes, too!
He takes her other hand, which she withdraws.
He tells her that the guys he plays with now
are pretty good, but they're not on the edge.
And another thing—he laughs—it smells
of coffee over here—great coffee, true—
but coffee, man. A pause. Now here it comes.

At least he has found her—what she once liked
to call *un coup de hasard*. There's no response.
He draws some screwy symbol in spilt beer;
it becomes the focus of his gravity.

He tells her that he brought her to Le Club
early tonight to thank her from springing him
from the booby hatch and for these last months,
and to tell her he's decided to go home
alone this trip, to Eisenhower, but not
to either ball & chain (The Prince has found
it smart to have a background wife or two).

She drains her glass, ignores his open palms,
then tells him that her girlfriend, Juliette,
called him a *diamant brut*—'a rough diamond.'
But in the end he's just the cocksure
Noir américain, another bastard man.
How sexy she can make even that sound,
his little existentialist. The door
lets out a cloud of warm air as she leaves.
Walking the Rue St. Benoit, the skyscrapers
of her imagination fade. She hears
his gravel tone and sees the ceaseless
movement of those hypnotic, loving hands.
And of the words he said to her just now?
She caught enough to gather she's been dropped.

He hangs around to drink another beer.
He's back in Harlem in the dirty snow
and playing the Apollo with a rhythm
section that's on loan from Jesus Christ.
And then—knock, knock—it all begins again;
the cops are backstage; another hassle.
Still, the Lord said fill thine horn with oil and go.
He will miss her. And Paris, too. In fact
this whole, ennobling European thing.
Tonight, the last time that we play together.
Well, fuck! At least he gave it to her straight.

IN WHICH HE ARRIVES IN THE BIG APPLE & MEETS HIS LADY OVER COFFEE

He brings her dope
He plays her ballads
Now what the fuck
Are all these salads?

He wonders what it is with chicks like her
that as soon as they get their painted toes
under the sheets they start to try to change him.
Like for instance: he's been with Marcie—what,
six weeks?—sharing her tiny palace
on West 127th Street (Her plumbing
is a rhythm section of its own)—
and she's already on his case: 'Ty darlin',
this stuff will kill you, if that stuff don't.
Eat this; fart that. Who was you lookin' at?'

A *coup de foudre* among the condiments,
they meet when he parked his ass on a stool
at Al's Luncheonette on Sugar Hill…

He's sitting doodling over donuts
waitin' for the dusk-to-dawners to come in,
a country boy just off the Richmond bus
with his tenor sax and fifty cent valise.
And one who yearns for 52nd Street—
the clubs, cat houses, clip joints and the like—
but first: he's heard that savvy cats hang out
at Al's, to plan their jams and shit like that.

Marcie is his waitress. She prowls around
and loads his cup and prattles on until
it's clear that he's the special of the day,
especially when she starts in moaning how

her G.I. fella's left her for Korea.
They bat the ball around. He says he never
likes to tango with the Stars and Stripes.
She asks him if he's scared, big guy like him.
He tells her if it comes to blows he's got
his ax right here. He counts to five (They don't
know puns from shit, these waitresses) and then
(double entendre aside, that is) it drops.

Shrill laugh. She claims her job is strictly rent,
that she's a singer just like Sarah Vaughan
(Why is it everyone is someone else?)
and starts to scat for him right then and there.
It's luck the place is old, empty and deaf
because the laugh is that she canNOT sing.
Poor Marcie is a waitress, end of tale,
this chick who's gonnna 'carve her name in riches
then retire'. He tells her, baby, in their world
the only way to wind up with a million
is to start with two. That sets her siren off.

He thinks it apt her name is Marcie Staines.
You can see it along the counter here:
coffee rings on rings—Fine-looking woman
though, this Marcie; buxom too. 'Apt'; 'buxom';
he likes such little flavors on his tongue.
That's one reason why he slipped the 'Prince'
between the 'Ty' and 'Dove'. Instinctively
he knows what isn't embouchure is image.

And speaking of those two, what's there to say
about those changes in Bird's solos, man!
Today he's out of luck; no yardbirds show.
She says she'll ask around; she knows Doc West.
But with the check he's down to seven bucks.

Guess what? She knows a place where he can crash…
It's time he taught himself Korean, *babo.*

HOW HE JAMS WITH BIRD & HITS THE WATER RUNNING

So what's he playing at? He drank too much
and now he's sweating like a bastard. Why?
Because he's just about to share the stage
with Bird—with Bird, right? At the Open Door,
a bar restaurant in the Village. A back room
jam session on a Sunday afternoon.

They tried him out an hour ago, gave him
some cockeyed riffs to play, some wild shit
the way they used to do at Minton's. He blew
them all away and now he gets to play
with that celestial, sure-footed cat
who can make even the loan sharks cry.

But this is some lugubrious venue, man,
a derelict ballroom with a bandstand
and woodpeckered tables. Lotta anxious dudes.
He's just back from the head a second time,
working his sorry way through smoke and sweat,
a haze of expensive booze and cheap perfume.
And then he gets the nod and it's his time.

Bird's blowing like a mother on 'Funky Blues',
the others falling all around him
as they try to milk the cat's inventiveness.
And one poor dodo's out to match him
note-for-note. Then suddenly the penny drops:
it's him. He is the flightless, fucking bird.
Angels and ministers of grace defend us.
Next thing a voice is chewing on his ear:
'Hey don't just do something, my man, stand there.'
The stage explodes in laughter and he's cooked.

He grovels on until the set is done
then makes a bumbling bee-line for the door,
at which he gets the nod from Bird, who waddles
over shoeless, Mister Five By Five—
he's two men in his suit these days—and then
that husky voice which heralds sermon time:

'Hey don't you know that it's respect that kills?
Be bold; be resolute—and don't play me.
You got to show what's in that bag of yours.
Like your tone's your own voice, man. My fucked-up
history is in those licks. You don't want that.'

He rolls his sleeves and shows his needle tracks.
'See there's my penthouse, that my Cadillac.
These tracks you're looking at, they don't lead home.
I heard that you got something, man. No shit.
You're hungry, right? Well no-one gives a fuck.
Until young Lady Luck comes wiggling her ass,
you may just as well play with yourself.

Now how about you spot me ten? No bread?
You mothers have got nothing but your balls.
Stay cool. I gotta go and hock this horn.
Ain't mine.' He rounds his shoulder with those eyes.
'And man, just keep your mouthpiece safe, is all.
Finesse the rest...and off I deliquesce.'

The Prince debouches into Washington Square—
among the pigeon shit and wino drool.
Did Bird really lay that sage advice
upon his regal head just now or is
he improvising on the nod he got?

He squares his shoulders, finds his strut, takes off.
One thing he's learned from listening to the man:
you gotta keep your reed hard for the jam.

WHEREIN HE WALKS THE BAR FOR BIG MAYBELLE

If music be the food of love he's out
two of the three, and so he finds himself
ass-deep in snowy Cleveland wailing blues
strictly for the spondulicks. He's pinch-hitting
for Trane who's stepping out again. The Prince
can rhyme internally but hardly sees
to blow that horn of his round Big Maybelle,
bless that ten gallon Tennessee heart of hers.

The first set's done; he's loosening his jaws
on why he took the old cold bus to town,
explaining how, when they are busy
pooling ninety seven cents and change
while sitting in their threadbare overcoats
at Bill's cold-water, Barrow walk-up
(which gets its heat at what are known as 'meal times')
Bam!—the cops burst in and find...not even
furniture. The landlord's picked it clean for rent.

Now where the cops do not discriminate
is in matters of possession of
narcotics; they'll put the cuffs on anyone.
Even so tonight someone's fucked up.
So full of confidence they'd find the junk
they didn't think to bring their own along
to plant. They snort and squeal but a void
like Bill's has nothing to regurgitate
and even when the four musicians stand
buck-naked in the empty room nothing
swings except their sticks. The bull cop prowls
and growls it seems it's their mistake this time.

Before the Prince can leash his bardic self
he's off on a favourite riff of his:
"'Seems", madam? Nay, it is; I know not "seems."
'Tis not alone my inky cloak, good mother—'
His windy suspiration of forced breath
is cut right there. They'd book him for recital
of Act 1 scene 2, if New York law allowed.

He lights a Lucky, ready to describe how
that misunderstanding led to here
when Maybelle waddles over. She wants
to know what all the shit about Shakespeare
she keeps hearing is. He tells her that the Bard
is in his genes. That gets a laugh all round.
She says she knows what's in his jeans; she wants
to have him walk the bar in the next set.

Walk the bar! Strut it, blowing his horn,
kicking over glasses, showing his chops.
The Prince is way above this sort of shit
but he can hear the whispering of greenbacks
clearer than the rustle of her skirts and so
he packs his monologue and grabs his ax.

Soon Maybelle's sack of jello's heaving
at the rowdy crowd—even the boys at stretch
can't hold her back. And then, his solo here,
the Prince drops roughly from the half-assed stage,
snakes through the smoke, hops up a makeshift stair
and there he stands: the sax and its colossus
on the bar. He blows and sweats and struts
as glasses squirt from underfoot, or crunch
beneath his giant step. They lap it up
these groundlings of the Buckeye state. Until,

that is, he pauses like a pachyderm
with one foot poised aloft. Ahead he's seen
this most unwelcome visitation:
a switchblade quivering in his path.

Either his eyes are made the fools of
other senses, or else he'd better split
or he can hop it like they did as kids
or he can stomp the guy who's looming up—
or how about he shows his horn's got
a reverse gear loud as any Sherman tank?
And so he blows backasswards
down the bar's beat-up mahogany,
everybody hooting, cheering, howling when
disaster strikes. His foot skids in a pool
of Bűrger beer that's settled in a gouge.
He sees his legs fly north as he heads south.

These nurses are no picnic either—
who the fuck likes fruit?—and they're so crazy
about cleanliness it stinks. The truth is
these dark ladies of the sonnet wonder
if his problem isn't an over-active
libido rather than the concussion
that doctor with the stammer diagnosed.
In his own considered judgment, the Prince
sees two of nothing—except maybe Maybelle.
And so, when left alone at changeover,
he collects his shit together in this starchy,
piss-ass ward and streaks for open country,
(Exeunt, he and the pursuing bear.)

AN AUDIENCE WITH THE PRINCE

He likes to huff and puff and blow the house down
but half the porkers in the audience
are from the Fleet and they're all busy
with not listening. Instead their vocal cords
are happily vibrating in the spirit
of the Constitution's First Amendment.

He side-mouths Red that what they've got is Circe's
crew out there tonight (drawing another
Homeric blank). So he has the quintet play
a vamp-till-ready while he's waiting on
a kind of hush that doesn't come, and then
he leans into the mike to try a pitch
he's told that Mingus made (All right, he's heard
it didn't work, but it will surely
mollify, and the Prince is right now
in the kind of mood his drummer, Red, would call
bituminous—if he availed himself
of metaphors as freely as he does of dope):

'Ladies, mariners, gentlemen, it's come
to our attention you're not getting
what you paid for, and we sure as shit
ain't getting your attention. You see
the Ty 'Prince' Dove Quintet are graduates
of academe and broken homes. So please
shut-the-fuck-up and listen and enjoy.'
He waits—the clamor's undiminished—
then rises up above it with, 'OK,
let's compromise. We play four bars; you talk four.'

And off they go. They play a chorus,
followed by a four bar break and then the Prince
waves out the band. He counts four measures
of the racket all around them; then they take
the next four…and on it goes. There's laughter
from the cognoscenti, while the Navy
jabbers on. One guy, though, who's sitting by
a hat-check girl he used to know, is up
and suddenly advancing on the stage.
This dude is like a trireme mast on legs.
(Where is Joe Louis when you need the cat?)

The Prince is big but pacifistic
like that Hindu sage, Gandhi. Behind him
are his crew of sissies, all called Sonny,
Blue, or Red. A .38 might do the trick
but these are strictly lotus-eating types
and all they shoot is dope. Besides he's knows
the quintet concept can evaporate
when heat's turned up. Like now when Birnam Wood
has suddenly arrived in Dunsinane.
It's down to him; it's Marshal Dillon time.

Is this guy reaching for a hide-away?
In a flash he sees the headline: 'Irate Fan—'
or wait—is this some showdown with a husband,
dealer, pimp—or cop? Could this be a bust?
Narcotics, alimony, repossession?

But what this guy pulls out is just a pen
a Parker pen. This sonofabitch
has scared him shitless for his autograph,
his anonym, his appellation.
Meanwhile his heart's been going like John Henry's
while beneath his fifteen dollar lime green shirt
his skin is slick as oleomargarine.

Later, as he wipes his neckpiece, scowling
at the oblivious members of his crew,
he puts tonight's fiasco down to moly,
to the pharmaceuticals he's ingested
on his watch. So it was Paranoia
not Poseidon after all. He can dig that.
But don't go telling him the Big Bad Wolf
ain't out there, because the Prince has seen its tracks.

OF HOWLING AT THE MOON & DIGGING
BILL EVANS

So Thomas Hardy was a meliorist?
He sure the fuck is not. If anything he's
up for barking, baying, howling at the moon
like that old schizo Pierrot in Debussy's
Cello Sonata. A meliorist?
Life is a crock of shit and that's the truth.
Take him, for instance. In this month alone:
an old flame went out in the Atlantic

      'Over the mirrors meant
      To glass the opulent
The sea-worm crawls—grotesque, slimed, dumb, indifferent.'

Plus, they've suspended his cabaret card
and he's having trouble with Shirelle—
his new Marcie—*and* the cat is AWOL
and his fifth floor walk-up's run by roaches.
Oh, and Rita Hayworth's married someone else.
So what the fuck's all this about Hardy?

Well listen: at the Colony last night,
a neighbourhood joint in Bedford Stuyvesant
('Not a nice place, really,' the English would say)
he's giving the ear to Miles' new sextet—
not out for crumbs or shit like that; in fact
he'd been doing all right at the Five Spot—
until they grounded his sax. He doesn't need
a handout; he's just watching Philly work.

Anyway, he meets this white guy, sits down
practically on his knee, not seeing him
through clouds of Camel smoke. Obviously
the guy's nervous—hey, who wouldn't be?
They're giving him Red Garland's chair next set.

So the conversation's trimmed as Shirelle's ass.
Plus, anyway, George Russell's with the dude.
(He's the deep cat who wrote a book he called
The Lydian Chromatic Concept of Tonal Organization.
He borrowed it one time to turn-on Marcie—
hell, the title would have been enough.)

It's only when this cat is up on stage
he clocks the name: Bill Evans. He has a way
of moulding to the piano and he plays
under the rhythm; there's poetry right there.
You can see that Miles is digging him.
They all are. This cat phrases just like Bird.

When the set is done they talk of this and that—
Debussy, Hardy—all those sheep and dales
and dairy maids and fate and shit. Like Brooklyn.
And then, when pressed, this cat articulates
the 'mission' that his music's taken on:
to put emotion into the piano.
What starts in technique ends in feeling.
OK, the Prince digs that. The way he talks,
the way he looks, he'd pass for one of those
young science guys. He could have been in on
'Explorer 1' or one of Einstein's stunts.

In point of fact he's almost too cerebral,
except that this is what the Prince requires:
someone who can quote from Thomas Hardy
and will bust his chops as well. Like the Prince.
This is a guy, George says, with bookcases!
A guy who reads Kafka, Sartre, Freud and Zen.
This is the kind of guy who plays piano
with Debussy sitting in his pocket.
He can see it now: classical jazz,
played by Ty 'Prince' Dove and plain Bill Evans.
(He'll bring the blues). He can almost hear

the purists moan, those dicks who like to think
that white musicians are a brand dilution.
That's jazz as coffee. You can serve with cream
but its natural flavor's black. Assholes!
Like Miles's, his thinking's light years ahead.
This white cat's offering something new.

One thing though: he needs to lighten up.
He listens too intently—they'll rib him raw.
See how tonight the Prince has stopped *his* howling;
that's self-restraint. The readiness is all.
What this cat needs is the Prince to be his guide.
(He'll need to spirit him away from Miles.)
They'll meet where Africa and Europe meet.
Shit, it'll be the Convergence of the Twain.

AFTER LOCKING HORNS WITH DEXTER

The Prince has blown his session with old Dex
literally and metaphorically.
He's come apart at the keys. What happened's
going round his head like Clark Terry's breathing...

He's got himself rekindled at the Five Spot
hard on the heels of Monk's shit-hot quartet
and a new squeeze, a nightclub camera girl,
but despite ecstatic solos he's in thrall
to a bout of Old DominionWeltschmerz
standing on 8th Avenue at 3 a.m.
waiting on a cab and wishing he could make
'The Ed Sullivan Show' like Benny Goodman
when who should pull up but Dexter Gordon
in a Chevy that's seen better paint jobs.
Dex doesn't uncoil his enormous length
right then and there, but leans   way out.

This is the legend who translated Bebop
into tenor sax and taught the way
of sartorial hip. He suit-ed Miles
a decade back and was indeed the glass
wherein the noble youth did dress themselves.
He greets the Prince with that warm West Coast smile,
saying how he likes the way he blows
and how about he brings his horn along
to the Prince's gig tomorrow for a toot?

There's the smell of audition in the air.
He'd heard that Dex was out of Folsom,
that he'd copped an East Coast date to cut some sides.
He must be here to try his chops against
a younger dude, a perilous way
of coming clean. Now the Prince knows all about

the bouts with Teddy Edwards, Wardell Gray
but they were years ago. Besides he's made
an art of thinking on his feet. And then
cutting sides and cutting Dex would spread
his name from this coast all the way to that.
He'd be moving up a weight like Sugar Ray.

And so next evening cometh the man
and natty entourage—to wild applause.
The excogitating Prince invites
his guest into the hurricane's single eye.
Blow, winds, and crack your cheeks! rage! blow!
For half an hour these mighty tenors two
stand trading haymakers, the crowd entranced,
for the horns of the righteous are exalted.

Perhaps it is the Prince on points. But then—
post-pyrotechnics—his old friend Dizaster
comes a-calling. They are melting hearts
with 'Cry Me A River' and Dex is basking
in that slow and breathy warmth of his
when the Prince is shocked to find himself naked-
ly, unstoppably weeping. Divesting
himself of his horn, he steps to the wall
while Dex plays on, stops to compose himself
before The New York Fire Department's
posted notice, then exits unobtrusively—
with every eye in the joint fixed on him.

The autopsy at 2 a.m. goes like this:
The Prince is standing wreathed in Lucky smoke
while Dex sits patiently, still affable
despite the Prince's earlier retreat.
Being mystified, he takes a stab. 'I think
that you did real well. But don't compromise
your talent playing with bums like these;
your rhythm section's lagging, man. I've played

with better bands while in the jug, and I
was healthier there, too. No cats to phone
me all day long, or stop me on the street.'
His voice takes on a crusty, wheedling tone,
'Hey Dex, my man, come on, let's swing right now.'
Then comes his trademark laugh, like Moby Dick.

The Prince's tragedy lies otherwise
and here it is without the candy shell:
he sprang a leak at one face in the crowd,
the mirror of his longago Daddy.
And so he plays his sorry tune for Dex
allargando. It concerns his father's death,
the coroner, his uncle's taking on
the matchbox roadhouse, marrying his mother
in unseemly haste and then in slow-mo
cheap-boozing himself to death, while the Prince
(plain 'Ty Dove' then) stands for centuries beside
the shabby juke box in their shady bar
playing with the music for loose change.

Dex, who has devoured whole libraries
while in the jug, reminds him that a guy
who takes the stage as Hamlet may bow out
as crazy as old Lear. Personal demons
man, they are a pain in the royal ass.
But then he plants this beautiful seed.
He tells the Prince he yearns for exile,
his motto: For hope without dope, choose Eu–rope.
Go mingle with the Gallic epicures
advises Dexter, scout the terrain
like that cool white cat in 'Wagon Train'.

IN PARIS, LOVING & SHRINKING

Everything, even this blindingly white room
with the iron bed and the bowl and the bars
into which they come and mostly go without
a word, even this conjures up Sabine.
She's on him like cologne, but where is she?
In their room at the Hôtel Louisiane
hanging out with the rhythm section
holding a joint and a *ballon de vin rouge*?
Or is she here in this nuthouse, trying
to persuade the shrinks he's been misunderstood,
that everyone's a little crazy sometimes?

He remembers trying to lose his clothes
to 'Body and Soul' right there on stage
and then the soulful gendarmes clomping in
batting him about the head, her chanting
liberté, égalité, fraternité
for reasons he is not entirely sure.
He remembers being slumped over the john
in the gendarmerie, puking up
the bennies and the booze in CinemaScope,
picturing his chick in tears, mopping up
his mind for the next set—what next set?—
then someone must have called for the white coats.
He's with a guy whose accent's making oatmeal
of the things he says—a shrink presumably—
a fan of Aaron Bridgers at The Mars Club, or
it could be Arrant Bitches at The Mouse Club.
Anyway he asks the Prince where he 'perfumes'.

The answer is—until last night at least—
at the Blue Note on the rue d' Artois.
He's working there with Kenny Clarke and French types.
He likes to lean against Klook's beat. (Max told him

that the cat went off to France to give the sticks
back home a chance). And then of course Sabine
is there, smouldering before him. The downside
is the rotgut wine he smuggles in
because he can't afford to patronise the bar—
the joint's a shoe box and they pay in dimes.
Still, it's Paris, so they play their asses off.

She walks right in one night, a few weeks back,
his *fille*, a blonde dressed to the eyes in black.
Maybe she's out to cause arrhythmia—
or else to poison apples. *Tout à coup*
his often almost-wedded heart's off-key.
He lets the bass player walk, gives her the eye
and she comes on to him in classic French:
with seventeen smile muscles unemployed.
He gives the nod to Klook who'd not be fazed
if existentialists stormed Notre Dame.
Yet even he's missing a beat. So then
he treats her to his princely, soulful licks
and by the time he wraps 'You Leave Me Breathless',
they are both in need of oxygen.

When the set expires he finds his fingers
phrasing on her table top and then—guess what?
They find they speak the same lingo: *pain*,
amour—that kind of thing—*Marlon Brando*
and not much else. Her American is wild.
At first they go to her place but the room
is in some backstreet shithole and anyway
it's too small for him to squeeze his body
in, leastways not so they can operate.
Instead they decamp to the Louisiane
where there's room to swing a *chat* or two.

While they're deep in congress that first time
she says this thing, Sabine, to him, this thing
he liked and which she later scribbled down:
Il n'y a que le premier pas qui coûte—
which means it's only the first step that costs.
He's heard she dropped out of the Sorbonne
to make her living out of tending bar.
Another time she quotes Pascal to him,
that we are like the *'gloire et rebut de l'univers'*—
the glory and the refuse of the universe.
He loves that kind of shit, because it's true.

It's in the stuff he plays and every
enamel bowl he fills. The shrink knows that.
It's in the rattling keys and warmest smile
with which he brings the news that Mademoiselle
has satisfied his colleague that the Prince's
wild behaviour is the product of excess—
of joy—at the news that she's knocked up,
and planning to go back with him stateside!
He's being released into her care. Right then
she rushes in, Sabine, effervescent
as a flute of Veuve Clicquot. He could swear
he's never seen her smile before. Is it
a sense of humor she's giving birth to?

He waits until they're through the wrought-iron gates
before enquiring what the fuck is going on.
'Bump,' she says, and laughs, making the shape
against her belly, then shakes her head.
And so the bump is gone. But the way Sabine's
all over him is worrying the Prince.
Is she confusing him with Uncle Sam?
It's only the first step that costs. Fat chance.
The Prince comes down to earth with his own bump.
His nights are numbered with this clued-up chick.

WHICH TREATS OF SABINE'S DREAM OF CAMUS WITH THE PRINCE PLAYING ALONG

The Prince is sauntering Saint-Germain-des-Prés
taking in the cellar clubs, bookstores, beggars
and remembering Jimmy Baldwin's words
that only his passport keeps him regal here.
True, but at night he's treated like an artist
not a horn-blower like they think back home.

In truth the Prince is rarely seen in daylight.
He's come to meet Sabine at Les Deux Magots.
Not 'maggots', surely? He's been in many
a roach-infested place but this ain't one.
His beer arrives with her and a pale face friend
who wears her coppery hair like Lassie's.
This is Éloïse who speaks American.
He loves those names—Éloïse, Sabine—
his own kid he would call Gethsemane,
Gethsemane Dove, bird in the garden.

The two are high on shopping and some dream
Sabine has wet herself to tell him of.
Before you can say Jack Roosevelt Robinson
she's off like a Coltrane solo, Copperhead
translating. All the big names: Camus, Sartre,
de Beauvoir and some guy called Koestler.
Anyway the gist of the dream is this:

These hotshots all roll in at midnight.
They've been dancing on the rue de Gravilliers
that dump with the neons, pink and blue.
Tonight the club is empty—it must be
the Prince's deadest gig since '52,
night of the Walcott v Marciano fight—

but guess what?—they make a beeline for Sabine.
Where is the Prince? Of course he's up there playing
and that's pretty much the last he figures
in her dream. He's never had to comp before—
maybe because this Al-Bear guy is cute,
though Sartre's like a toad and the woman bony.
The other's a fiery short Hungarian.
They mostly talk at once which is a way
of going out together on your own.

Apparently he's partway through a set
when the place erupts, drunken thinkers
flying everywhere. Then Fernandel
comes lumbering by and ejects the lot.
Sabine pauses. The Prince is waiting
for some punchline; Paleface is smirking.
The joke is in what kicked the ruckus off
and he would put a sawbuck on Sabine.

So here comes Koestler in his croaky French
complaining they are dumb as Chukchi huskies
because 'on Stalinism you are soft'.
And since he doesn't share their politics,
they can kiss his butt as far as friendship goes.
They all tut (it's a European thing).
Koestler scowls but Camus is beaming bubbles
of cheap vodka and champagne the while,
saying friendship is above that kind of crap.
De Beauvoir is nodding sagely, while Sartre
is just too drunk and anyway engaged
in rehabilitating pocket lint.
Then someone knocks a drink across them all
and everyone's in tears, though not for that.
It's for lost love—or *La condition humaine*.

To cheer them up Sabine gives out her line
about Man being the glory and the refuse
at which Sartre drops a thread, announcing
we *are* the refuse, each of us alone
but Camus claims with moral values
we'd achieve the *gloire*. Someone says it's Sartre
who is the refuse, and that's when someone
throws a sucker punch—maybe de Beauvoir;
it's a bony hand. But it could have been
the mean one, Koestler, because he ups
and overturns the joint and out they go.

While the three of them are strolling along
Bonaparte—another toney rue—
the Prince is thinking how he's never heard
at length what's going off in Sabine's head
though she's fixed herself like Elmer's Glu-All close.
(Klook reckons Diz once told him he'd use
Elmer's on him if he dropped another stick.)
He tells Sabine that she's become his Muse.
'Muse, my ace,' she says, with a playful push.
'She means my ass,' says Éloïse. 'My ass
is what you say.' And off their sirens go.

Too many dogs about. And just before
he's pushed in one, the Prince is thinking how
he'd have been at home among the blowhards
of Sabine's dream. You play joints that don't have mikes
you soon learn to blow out like Dex. Besides
though oft times the Prince obscures his contemplation
under the veil of wildness, he's one deep dude.
Why just this week he's been gray mattering
with Richard Wright in the Romance Bar—
that's where the cat hangs out—on whether Paris
is a refuge or a revolution.
The Prince can brain it with the best of them,
but his Sorbonne's the Sax. Meanwhile he's scraping
surreptitiously this shit off of his shoes—
before that cracks his two chicks up as well.

ON BEING BACK AT BIRDLAND

He's sitting there, blowing hot and cold:
To quit or not to quit. He's Hamleting.
These cats wouldn't know an autodidact
from a car mechanic. Pres died today.
He's wetting his reed, waiting out the time
in a shoe box dressing room, wallpaper
foxed as an old Bible. Well, shit happens.

He's still hearing from her—mostly harangues—
but though the whole Paris scene's six months back
French rumours turn the management uptight.
Right now he's back and bad as ever was,
playing Birdland soberish most nights
and yet can only recruit also rans.
Apparently he has a reputation
to live down. Hence the suicidal itch.
Besides, these junkies make him paranoid.
So what, he can't just blow and stash the gelt?

That's not his style. He lights a Gauloise.
It freaks the hell out of his undertakers.
French reefers, they call them. He has a hatful
of the real thing; joints for a joint like this.
Drinking cold coffee from a paper cup,
his fingers could circumnavigate twice.
Now circumnavigate's a billfold word,
a hooker right at home among these gaudy
gilded cages. He should just turn up and blow.

Pres had his own language, his own style:
called the cops 'Bob Crosbys', old girlfriends 'Waybacks'.
Had his own way of doing things, for sure.
A man that fortune's buffets and rewards…

the cat would crack you up. That midget mc—
that irritating little shit, the nasal one
with the falsetto—Pee Wee? Pres once called him
'half a motherfucker'. And another thing:

he wants it tattooed right across his ass
he will not play 'The Way You Look Tonight'
again tonight. He's playing with morticians,
gravediggers who bury what they don't embalm.
Il ne faut pas fatiguer le public, she'd say.
Well, Paris is sprinkled with fairy dust;
they couldn't get enough of him back there.
He had it all: Sabine, respect—the shrink.
He balls the empty pack; rolls it; crushes it.
He should go back. What was he thinking of?
Fuck the divinity that shapes our ends.
Maybe tonight, in memory of Sabine,
he'll open with 'More Than You Know' and then
for all the chicks before Shirelle he'll close
with 'How Long Has This Been Going On?'

So he's making bread; blowing well. What's more
to want—except to make himself *au fait*
with what's been going on while he's been gone?
Maybe he'll call on Miles, sit in on Trane
or Newk. The Pres is dead. Long live the Prince—
but not this asshole Prince Procrastinator.

WHERE HE SINGS THE BLUES FOR LADY DAY

He's rehearsing with his new quartet, right?
But the drummer's all over everywhere.
So he's asking him where the fuck the beat lies
when Red comes in with the news that Billie's dead,
Billie Holiday. The beat stops right there.
He knew that she was back in hospital
and that she'd been arrested for possession
of narcotics in her goddamned bed.
But dead? He wonders what it is with God
that first he snatches Pres then gallops back
for Lady Day. Thrift, thrift, Horatio.

He knew her on and off when she was living
at the Wilson. He had a chick lived there.
All three of them were into Chinese food.
They had a poky restaurant next door.
Billy lived on boiled rice and getting high;
she lived on Gordon's gin and Seven-up.
She also had a pimp who kept her poor.
On top of that the courts liked nothing more
than cutting up her cabaret cards.
And even when she could find work, the clubs
would claw some money back by hiring
local pick-up bands to play with her.

Europe might have saved her ass, or at least
her self-respect. In Paris he'd liked being called
Le Noir américain. It pealed regally.
He might be black, but he was treated white—
and they threw in the 'American' as well,
which they sure as shit begrudge back home.
But they booked old Billie badly over there
and then the bastards turned around and axed
her tour. She had to work her passage home.

So what they had in common, then, was Pres,
that and a little flavoured rice. He even
spotted her a C note once when he was flush.
She kept her distance, though, given his rep.
One time she said this thing to him, she said
'When I wear lacy pants, you'll be the first
to see 'em, Prince. Till then just keep that sweet tongue
and them endless fingers on that sax of yours.'

He'd seen her last his first week at the Five Spot.
She looked a mess; she'd come on by to score.
His head, however, had been in…Elsinore.
Maybe he gave her cab fare, maybe. No
not even that. It's a hole in his heart
this morning, having to remember that,
what with his fucked-up drummer reminiscing
now Red has bought the news of her demise.

'Demise.' She'd like that word; she'd call it class.
Because her life was mostly just being trashed
or tying tourniquets. She must have played
a thousand joints that wouldn't let her in
except as hired help. All those cheap hotels,
side doors and clubs she couldn't buy a drink in.
It's only natural she'd cling to any
little whiff of class that blew her way,
especially with that hard luck voice of hers.
Eat shit your whole life long you're in for a whole long life.
Then weigh a little courtesy like 'Lady'
against all that and suddenly you're regal.
You become a thoroughbred of disdain—
a fragile one. He knows about that, too.

He's on a riff now, at the window there,
taking a time-out, looking down on garbage.
He lights a joint and holds the fire inside.
You've not to wait for the Last Judgment;

it takes place every day (That's good old Al-Bear).
So if he gave her fuck-all that last time
well that's on him! We all father regrets.
All the perfumes of Arabia.
Regret is hard to swallow, just like race—
except regret's a true democracy.
But Lady Day has gone and she could sing.
He takes the joint in little sips and smiles.
Shit, that's the truth, her singing, that's the truth.

WHEN THE PRINCE IS MILES AHEAD

There's no-one better at blowing his own horn,
but right now he's rusting between gigs.
While Miles is busy playing Birdland
with an eye-popping lineup built for speed
'The Prince of Sax' is playing with himself.
Which is why he listened to that little voice
inside his glass last night that whispered
how, if Trane is pulling out, then Miles
might have a spot for him already warm.

As he breathes in August's woolly air, hungover, loping along Lenox Avenue,
the car keys in the pocket of his pants,
his mind is firing sluggishly. For one:
Where did he leave the fucking car? And then:
How is he going to square the thing with Miles?
For the Prince himself has been about a piece
of iniquity. What's also nagging
is the line-up of his next quartet, and then
there is that chick swinging ahead. He stops
to think…if Philly's been cut loose, then—
a guy whose name he'd scraped off of his shoe
a long way back suddenly appears.
'I thought I heard you was in Paris, man?'
He was, but now he's back, to Cold War rhetoric,
the S.I.N.A. and I Love Lucy.
He gives the guy a look: still an asshole.

So why did he come back to this shit hole?
He tries 'concatenation', 'sidereal'
and gets a grin homey as old bubblegum.
'Same old Prince. How were those French girls
over there, man?' 'Lubricious.' The old ghost

weighs the sound and nods his head. 'Hey listen:
d'you hear that Miles was beaten by some cop?'
Give the Prince Paris any day because
life is a demented chess board over here.

He drops the guy a joint and turns off Lenox.
The chick has disappeared meanwhile. Heigh-ho.
A kind of rebirth is what his ass needs.
Maybe tonality is a dead-end street—
he's startled by a sudden horn. Fucker.

And so he paid the call on Miles last night.
The cat has a Tenth Avenue apartment
and a new lady in his life, a dancer,
plus a white Ferrari convertible
which must have cost at least $8000 bucks.
Has a wrapper round his head. Still pissed off,
naturally. His little hoarse voice. 'My man!'
He might be firing, but he ain't hiring.
Besides, first up there's Sonny. The Prince knows
it would have been atomic egos, anyway.
Miles slips him this instead, this pointed yarn:

'Goodstein says the band ought to wear uniforms.
Everybody's doin' it; it's in the air—
in the fuckin' air!—So we come on stage,
the sextet, same regular clothes—But
I have a rack of matching suits brought on.
I say to the audience, "The management"—
get this!—"the management tell me you all
want to see uniforms; so we've brought you some.
You can sit and enjoy looking at 'em'
and we're just gonna leave you to it now.'"

Raspy laugh. 'You get it, Prince?' *Tout à fait.*
'Be your own man. Think big. This is Nietzsche shit—
The Übermensch. You're above their petty rules.'
The audience is at an end. He sneaks one
lingering look at Frances as he stands,
observes his own magician's fingers
at the door. And with that he steals away.
Gravelly laugh to himself in the lobby
Be your own man. You're above their petty rules.
Tosses in one manicured hand the keys
to a white Ferrari Chick-Cruiser.

Later he' dreaming of the Club St. Germain:
Mesdames et Messieurs, it gives us pleasure
to present for your delectation
at this time, *'Le Noir américain Quartet'*.
On tenor sax—and smart as a mother—
Le formidable Ty 'Prince' Dove. On drums:
Philly Joe Jones. On bass: the wunderkind,
Freddy Wilhelm Nietzsche. And on trumpet
and sincerely steamin': one Miles Davis.'

ENTER AS PRINCE

'Astronomically speaking, what you are about to hear is the birth
of a star: tenor saxophonist Ty 'Prince' Dove.' (from the "Sinful
Mood" liner notes)

The Prince is busy defying augury.
He's at the door and looking out of it—
both literally and metaphorically—
hungover, waiting on the other two
while the drummer's busy snorting rim shots.

He's back recording for Columbia
at that old church on 30th Street
on a quiet afternoon in fall.
The place is blessed with lots of wood
which makes for a good acoustic feel
and it has those warm Telefunken mikes.
But the session's just about to start
with two cats shy: piano man and bass.

In this same studio, six months before,
he played the beginning of a set with Miles
(their contretemps sorted with an uppercut).
His first flat note, his first clam came in just four bars.
An hour on and there was seashore all around.
Ah but then came the epiphany.
Listen and his solo builds from fragments;
then there's that pause before the modal shift—
a little dissonance, a little Africa.

A far cry from Africa but mixing
with the rocket fuel and worry in his head
is Rachmaninoff's 'Prélude in C-sharp minor'
and what he really loves about the piece
is its spare sound, the way the Russian works
with silence, like Miles, like the Prince himself.
Rachmaninoff lived in memory
because the guy was homeless half his life.

Ditto the Prince. It's like Hawaii
and Alaska are now both states and both
are more at home. This horn is where he lives.
Dex and Trane, Mobley, Rollins, Jimmy Heath—
internal exiles every one of them.

The Russian reckoned he'd earned $20
for that score. The Prince's rhythm section
will make more than twice that for the session—
if they show. It gave him clout to come here
though he might have gone to Paris, like Bechet—
like Powell, like Dex, like the Prince himself
whose name will soon be storming Downbeat polls.

He's about to set fire to the songbook.
Cole Porter can kiss his ass. It's his turn
to take that 'rising star of Gotham' shit
and those liner notes that bristle with
$5 adjectives. He's something new.
Listen to him take the pickax to himself,
explore within. He thinks of Langston Hughes:
'My soul has grown deep like the rivers.'
It's time his sweat leaked back into its roots.

And on that note: what's with Shirelle these days?
Even the Pepsodent jingle caused a fight
and now she's thrown him out, redecorated.
He should return to Paris; breathe croissant air;
look up Sabine. What could possibly go—
bap! bap! bap!—they're here at last. Stay cool!
The clock is chewing dollar bills; let's roll.

The English call it barking mad, this urge
to put oneself through shit, time and again.
Yet what can he—most sleek and quarrelsome—do
other than cement his reputation as
            The Prince of Cats.

The Noir American has offered me a chance to play among the jazz men and women of the 1950s and to steal some of the wonderful anecdotes about them. Although it is essentially comic, the poem is meant with great respect.

Ty 'Prince' Dove is a fictional tenor sax player, an egotistical autodidact obsessed by 'Hamlet'–and the dignity that Paris offered to his generation of African-American artists. His immediate origin is in a line from Bertrand Tavernier's 1986 film, 'Autour de minuit'/ 'Round Midnight'. In that film Dexter Gordon plays a broken-down saxophonist. At one point a female cleaner in a Parisian psychiatric hospital tells the friend searching for him: 'They didn't tell you there's a black American. He's in the annexe there.' Her 'Noir américain' gave me just the touch of alienation that I felt I needed for my character.

Or as the Prince might say (with his eye on the 'joint'):

'The time is out of joint. O cursèd spite,
That ever I was born to set it right!'

(Act 1 scene 5)

Other Lyrics

WORMS: A LOVE POEM

Last night in bed you asked if I could hear
faint gurgling noises from the yard next door,
my hearing being the flavour of the week.
'It's from Dipak and Raneesha's pool,'
you said. 'And the rain on the window pane.
I suppose you can hear that now at least?'
'Of course,' I said in the silence of the room.

This morning I ask you if you can see
how the grey that filters through the blinds
makes a lunar landscape of our quilt.
'Go on,' you say, 'is this about last night?'
I huff. 'I bet you can hear the light come in.'
'No, but blackbirds have been listening
on the lawn and they've started drumming their feet.'

TO IAN STEVENS IN HEAVEN

Ian, I took my title from a poem I like
    by William Carlos Williams

to tease you with my fond irreverence.
    I tell you this up front because
you who liked to construe the ancients
    feared to misconstrue the modernists.
Has your Pascalian wager paid off now?
    Who worries today about
the state of their soul, or feels the fraud you did
    despite your Oxford years?
The mildest, kindest and least confident
    of men. A soul ever damaged
by childhood disapproval, bolstered
    only by the affection
of those who took the time to know you
    though it seemed never quite enough.

A teacher who should not have taught
    whose size and lowered voice
seemed sinister (so your classes
    would sit silently
even when you hadn't left the staffroom
    where you kept your slippers
and always a loaf of white, sliced bread).
    Never in possession of your timetable:
'If they line up outside I bring them in to teach'
    (your George Medal lesson was well-aired).
In your ancient Ford one time I swore I saw
    the road beneath, delighting you
who loved old, battered cars and drove
    out of your way to avoid right turns.

The time I came to your bungalow
    I remarked on a box
of fish fingers wedging open an inner door.
    'Thawing nicely, lad', you said.
I didn't stay to eat but sat to hear you talk
    about your private passions:
steam trains, translating ancient Greek
    and Sundays playing the church organ
(partly to hedge your bets and partly
    to 'put an hour in', as you liked to say).
I have here a tattered, second hand King James
    you customised for me
with passages underlined in red, the ones
    you enjoyed reflecting on.

Ian, I like to imagine you, patiently
    in line behind a clutch of scribes
and hirsute Pharisees, waiting at the High
    wrought-iron gates of Heaven
for entry into the blessèd Kingdom
    and then being ushered in to Glory
where there are no classes, no need of courage—
    and, sadly, no ancient Greeks.

BENNY GOODMAN

for John Lucas

My favourite Bill Crow anecdote concerns
one '40s night in Princeton… Having set
the bandstand up for Benny Goodman,
his band boy noticed that the 'The King of Swing'
was low on smokes. Now privately they called
their boss 'The Ray'. The boy knew he would get
the glare, unless he found a pack and quick.

Not knowing where in the hell he was,
he asked directions off some white-haired bum
in baggy pants and sweatshirt, who quizzed him
on his hip couture—the yellow cardigan-
jacket, the pegged pants and beret—as if
he'd come from outer space. But he got the where
of a candy store and fluffed the old guy off.

Coming back he saw them crowding for the gig.
One kid broke off, came over, asked him what
'The Professor' talked to him about. 'Listen,'
said the band boy. 'Me and Mister Goodman
talk 'bout everything under the sun. Know why?
The guy's a genius.' 'No, I mean just now.
'What did old Professor Einstein have to say?'

BARBARY COAST

'I just decided I'd look better illustrated,'
says the young, piratical barber with the weights
dangling from his earlobes and the shock of black hair,
about the wealth of coloured tattoos up his arms.
'Expensive?' I enquire. His friend's a tattooist,
he explains, tries out ideas on him like the tiger
on his chest, or the porthole-polo on his elbow.

I think of Martin Amis' phrase 'self-vandalised',
but that's unworthy of a man so tirelessly
attentive to male grooming and so relaxed about
'the biz' (though he loves the superheroes clinging
to one arm). 'And your wife?' 'Her tatts are nautical:
galleons, sailors, a mermaid.' Laughs. 'Andy based
the lower part on a mackerel—don't tell her.'

Done at last, he scrutinises his performance,
flourishes my cape and sets me free. 'If my beard
was silver like yours is, I'd grow it way down here
like Gandalf's.' I chuckle with him, then overtip,
though one shouldn't look elitist at 'Elite Haircuts'.
He shows me to the door, says, 'Right then. Keep in touch.'
I'd like to think I would, but then I don't get out so much.

SOMME

He palmed the rouge
of his ten franc Marianne
and then in three weeks
when the huge
bombardment began
he worked it in his cheeks
to boost the confidence of his men.

The good Lord favoured neither her nor them.

TRAILWALKING AT CHANCELLORSVILLE

No glint of ghosts out here today,
no gripe or grumbling in these snarled
and silent woods, no smell of dough
on ramrods browning over fires

just live oak and loblolly pine,
this hellish heat, the drone of flies
and from the sibilance of tyres
along Route 3 to Fredericksburg

an echo of the rush of souls
escaping as the world expires.

WITH MICHAEL MOTT AT GAINES'S MILL

'It was as if in comradeship we found an affirmation of life and
the means to preserve at least a vestige of our humanity.'
– Philip Caputo *A Rumor of War*

We're passing through the ghosts of Hood's Texans
out of the friendly shade of beech and live oak
into the fierce heat of a Virginia day,
picking our way up from this piddling creek
from which they came to break Fitz John Porter's lines.
Summer's hum is startled by a crow;
a salamander flickers across our path.
Boys again, we're fired by thoughts of 'civil' war,
but can flags and costumed courtesies
disguise the fifteen thousand fallen here?

Just momentarily it seems. You pause
beside the cannon, against a split-rail fence,
sweeping the straw hat from your white hair
in an antique pose of exhortation
for my camera. We move at the sight of
a burly ranger ticketing my hire car
in the disabled spot of the Watt House
car park. Having failed to hang your permit
you adopt a feeble gait these last few yards.
We take our dressing-down with tongue-in-cheek.

Emerson saw no need to treat friendship
'daintily', but with 'roughest courage'. Ours
has become more robust with age, its English
reticence enlivened by your anecdotes,
our shared obsessions and three thousand miles.
How many briefer intimacies died out here?
Our lamplit friendship flickers beside
the blazing campfires of their comradeship.
They flit, restless in my imagination—
friend seeking friend—through this Virginia day.

THE PHEASANT

for Dan & Jen

Driving the country road in sun and rain,
carrying smoke and mirrors from the wedding
(wicker hearts and candles, gypsophila
and white roses, a thousand photographs
to light the hall's stone passageways)

arcing over the lane ten feet ahead
in a burst of flaming colours
a pheasant whirrs up from the hedgerow
like a second's sleight of bride and groom,
a hymn.

ANNIVERSARY POEM FOR TINA

40 years ago we met for our first date
on Central Library's stately steps.
We were 20 years before the mobile phone
and you were 40 minutes overdue.

Today we have outlived the library
which has discarded the encumbrance
of 400,000 books in the interests
of modern ignorance, for a reality
more virtuous for being more virtual.

For all the years of our married life
your patience has been as warming
as your openness. Lover and loved wife,
you're as much my measure as my good luck,
one who—to use an obsolete expression—
can read me like a b00k.

LAP

The lap only exists
when we sit.
So war-mongering Marcus Cato
shaking the lap of his gown
let fine figs

drop

saying to the admiring senators

they grow strong
    and ready
not three days sail from Rome

in Carthage
which lay lapped
by the blue Punic gulf

until the Senate rose to its feet.

CARTHAGE

There are no asphodels, no violets, no hyacinths;
how then can you talk with the dead?
   – George Seferis

Rock salt
sewn in fields dead of birds.
Here and there a flurry
of blown ash, ripped wool,
goat ribs and potsherds,
blood rust on rubble.

Sea salt
in the mouths of broken harbours,
in the charred beams of wrecks,
on the cracked lips of land
where once we listened
to the asphodels.

AT SKERRYVORE

R.L.S. admires Sargent's completed portrait of the Stevensons, 1885

Sargent! Thank God you're here old man.
Sit down. Who let you in? Ah, did she? Good.
    In truth I heard the door, but when
my work is going ill I've spirits that
    become quite subterranean.
Yet your arrival is an instant torch—
    and what is more you've brought the portrait,
splendid fellow that you are. Please, sit down.

    I'll hang it here I think—no, here
beside the small Venetian mirror
    Henry James presented us.
We identify Grandfather's armchair
    more with James—to use my favourite
adjective—after his frequent visits.
    Just as I will think of you,
whenever the portrait takes my eye.

    Yes, I will surely hang it here
so that all coming to visit us
    may admire me in my slow decline.
Now that's a work I'm well engaged upon
    if this past winter's any judge.
It's been a time of haemorrhages, chills,
    of influenza, fevers, pains—
more than I ever thought I'd live to bear.

    Your vision of this house of mine,
Old Skerryvore, is just as I might paint
    had I your Art. And what exquisite work
you make of dining room, and stairs,
    and of my pacing self! For as you know
This place is Denmark. Here is where I
    conjugate the cursèd verb *s'ennuyer*,
as Byron said. Damn health and property!

Well, what of that to this, this Art.
I think it wonderful, the atmosphere;
        I genuinely do. Of course
as there's no art to find the mind's construction
        in the face—the antecedent's
Juvenal, I think—one may just ponder
        why my portrait should be wanted
by the patron Fairchilds of the world.

        But you, you capture my condition;
you cage me just as I am caged. Bravo!
        You've put me in a mood to play,
your silence being an armchair of itself.
        Though do beware; you'll need a quip
when Fanny sees the portrait that you've done,
        the way you swathe her, cap-a-pie,
in ghostly sari at the canvas' edge.

        We're barely in the frame as one,
the two of us. You know she'll see this as
        some vindication of her itch
to think she's undervalued here. Not true
        of course, but women brood—Look, quick—
while Fanny is upstairs—let's toast the sex.
        No, you alone; drink's banned for me.
'To girls with pretty ankles and broad grins.'

        It's not for me to say you might
propose the toast yourself, my friend, being free
        of any woman's 'yeah or nay'.
You know, it's only Love in Life that will
        astound a man. Of course he'll set
about domesticating it until
        routine alone is left, which is
to leach the plumage of that gorgeous bird.

So should one turn to Art instead?
Dear James would have it Fiction can compete
    with Life on equal terms. But Art
can never do so much. No Art is true,
    if what we mean by Life is this:
the flavour of your wine, this lunchtime's sun.
    Sweet quickening of pulse are what
we get from Art; from Life: exquisite pain.

    At least the portrait is superb;
I think it is. Damned queer, but full of wit.
    I love the modulated tones
and Fanny disappearing in her dress.
    Indeed let's court the good opinion
of my sulking Muse. You can't imagine
    anyone who's so impatient
to be free of all constraints save her, as I.

SEEING ROBERT LOWELL PLAIN

Primed by professors I came to hear him read,
peered down upon a greying shock of hair
to catch that strange patrician Boston voice
risen from the fugitive South intone,
'I saw the spiders marching through the air.'
It took me ten more years to find the thread.

Lowell hoped his poems were heartbreaking
and wondered could there be forgiveness for
the waste of life pursuing the lifework.
Does distance free the poetry from its cost?
I learned to prize what salvaged from the wrecks,
that net of tarry rope nailed to the wall.

THE CRITIC

Tell me who loves, who admires you, and I will tell you who you are.
– Charles-Augustin Sainte-Beuve to Adèle Hugo

Rich, coppery, sudden coils of hair
sway to my waist. I do not miss a beat
as I address him in the glass. 'Oh! But
you mustn't leave the room,' I counsel him,
fixing his startled look with steady eyes.
'I'll pin it back in a moment. See.'

He had seen already, or thought he saw
at the unfortunate fall of the comb,
that our volatile poet's neglected wife
was no marmoreal Madonna with
a soul of marble, but Venus in disguise.
'The limbs of the Goddess,' he murmured,
scurrying after me into the garden.

We were hopeless lovers, heavy-thighed
about our ardours. After a time he read
the source of my silences as diffidence,
when it was really horror. As for him,
my disenchanted critic, nothing
ever moved in him again but words.

THEATRE

Take for example that long, lamp-lit
last moment at the end of *The Seagull*:
the doctor stands at Konstantin's desk
pretending to be absorbed in reading.
Trigorin is bent to kiss the actress,
Arkadina, to distract her from
the pistol shot off-stage which Dorn has just
dismissed as a bottle of ether
exploding in his old medicine chest
but was, in fact, the suicide
of her distracted son, Konstantin.
Shamrayev and Polina hold the look
they have exchanged, while Masha's fingers
lace her cheek. I close my eyes against
the house lights and the actors selling out
their characters for a handful of applause.

NIGHT CLOSURE

I'm up and down the M62 these days,
to visit Mother biding her decline
in a residential home in Huddersfield.
She meets her daily humiliations
with inattention, while I turn inside out
for family news to try to pass the time.
Recently I've wondered what one owes
a mother, beyond forgiveness, company.

Driving home I'm startled into swerving
to avoid a sudden duck and ducklings
walking arrow-straight and unperturbed
across my lane. Alert again, I watch
for signs. All are warnings. Three hundred
vehicles have been recovered on this stretch
of motorway the past three months alone.
Ahead there's notice of a night closure.

THE ISLE OF THE DEAD

On the turntable the end
of Rachmaninov's Op 29.

It is the last breath,
the shivering toward silence.

It is the sigh in the cypress
and Charon's exhalation.

What follows is the needle scratch
of oars on gloomy, glassy water

as the craft glides into the bay
below the abandoned temple

and one enters the hearth-cold death
of monophonic silence.

THE CRY OF CRANES

He is the worst of company, the lees this morning.
Drink once painted each drab day in noisy colours,
but now that brandy and cigars have been prohibited
what is their absence but an amputated limb?

The boatman hums a nursery rhyme of Iva's:
'Round the rocks... Round the rocks...' round the rocks this foam
looks nothing more nor less than beer lacing a glass.

Having torn to shreds what little he achieved this week
in his life and death struggle with the symphony,
he has fled the stillness with a fishing rod,
for the rocking ostinato of this skiff.

All silence is a poor rehearsal for Kuolema
which is why he listens for the cry of cranes,
their flute and oboe are his life's leitmotiv.

When one comprehends how little is achieved,
one comes to see how commonplace the talent
and that each name is simply scribbled there on water—
videlicet: Sibelius, off Järvö, 1910.

NEWHAVEN

A note that comes by air
brings a sea breeze:
your postcard hot from Philadelphia,
a salt print from an 1840s
calotype by Hill and Adamson.

And there he stands, James Linton,
proud as punch, one arm
propped on his boat proprietorially—
three urchins in its lee—
one hand on hip.

You've sent, in contrast, an apology
without show or swagger.
'Overwhelmed right now,'
your message reads. You mean it
as a bookmark in our correspondence
to signify that though you're currently
at sea, you'll come about.

I looked up 'haven' for its forebears:
Old English, Old Irish, Old Norse.
Who is it never needed sanctuary?

Let me wish for you, old friend,
your own new haven:
a shelter for the spirit, a salve
for ill health and a father's fears.
At least come visit us in England.
Here you'll find, if not a breeze,
a little breathing space.

IN AN ENGLISH COUNTRY GARDEN

for Kevin McCarter

Having no more sense at sixty-seven
 than at six or seven
I have discreetly ignored the rat
 because of my neighbour,
Clapton, for whom garden life is sanctified
 and who tolerates
an infinite variety of creeds,
as well as from a certain delicacy
 of my own, I'll admit,
at the sordid prospect of taking life

and so for weeks the rat we first encountered
 at Clapton's party
which he introduced as a bachelor
 and welcome presence—
even as his tawny cat studiously
 stared at the dogwood—
we too indulged him in our negligence
until the day we saw four, scuttering
 along our garden fence
nibbling at the azaleas and hebe

at which juncture you picked up the phone
 to call pest control
who arrived with three polite, white sachets—
 lethal within ten days—
and so today, day nine, I stand observing
 Papa Rat's fat backside
as he files his teeth on a border sleeper
looking, in our English country garden,
 as innocuous
as an old, discoloured tennis ball.

A DEATH FOR CAPTAIN CAREY

Captain Jahleel B. Carey, South Regiment, of unfortunate history
in Zululand, has died under mysterious circumstances in India.
(*The Army and Navy Gazette*, 1883)

I have dressed the Temperance Society tent
as you have advised me. It thrives, except among
the subalterns who, to a man, exist on pluck
and brandy. I live on tea, which should have meant
that I was proof against the agues brought on
by sleeping out at the field station. No such luck!

Ill health would seem to be as much my forte
as ill fortune. Well, pain is mortal, Father,
and now cholera bowls like a corrupt breeze
through the regiment. The air of Karachi may
stink like Philoctetes's wound, but I rather
look to the bazaar as the source of much disease.

The provisions they bring in, jellies and such,
will as quickly foul as feed a man's appetite.
I have closed the kitchens today. Mundified
them, as it were, but India is India; much
that is noisome, yet also so many delights—
culinary aside—it can hardly be denied.

Certainly the court martial sounded my knell.
'Cashiered but for his small force and good character.'
Father, you may applaud that last sentiment
but what of 'having had other duties as well
as command of the escort'. Did that register?
It means I'm sent to Coventry in the regiment.

Time and again in my sick bed these weeks past
I have tried my conduct from diverse perspectives
on that fateful day at the kraal. Here I squat,
there the Heathen crawling through tambookie grass
while I indulge the insouciant Prince, who gives
his orders languidly as we conduct our chat

about the virtue of his revered Great Uncle's
tactics at Borodino. I am enamoured
of his name when what I should do is demand
we all be on the *qui vive*. This Louis bungles
because he is inexperienced, too well bred
and loses his stirrup as he gives command

for the patrol to mount. Three of God's creatures lost
to negligence—which is a kind of innocence.
The court martial was just. I see at last why
I must take responsibility, accept my cross:
I was morally in charge. I failed through deference.
And then to have to leave a Prince behind to die!

Forgive me, Father. Do have joy of your hams
and thank you for the books. I envy the worldly spirit
of Browning's prelate (a *bon viveur* like yourself).
A pity he cannot meet our cook, this 'Blougram';
the fellow is still shaping fishcakes in an armpit.
And now a paradox: my brackish glass delivers health.

CASANOVA

He turns on to Oranienburger Strasse,
where late afternoon sunlight rubbles the vacant lots,
illuminating Berlin's love affair with tattered posters and graffiti.
He knows, come early evening, the slim prostitutes
in fancy corsets will line the street here.

He remembers forced and fumbled rendezvous twenty years before
in damp stairwells with a worried neighbour.
Today he fantasises an assignation more open,
more in keeping with the zeitgeist:

At Checkpoint Charlie, by the Brandenburger Tor,
beside the Roman Market Gate of Miletus,
by the blue and ochre tiled Persian Gate of Ishtar
or in the Lustgarten, where earlier he watched a girl
wrap her thigh around the pole that held the sign,
pretending to lick it for a girlfriend's camera.

Once he was a 'somebody', an IM, an informer.
Outed, he now posts bills to pay his way,
serves at a snacks counter near the Pergammon.
Now the wall is down, now 'Wir sind ein volk',
he has nothing to report, nothing to barter.
Now everything is out in the open
and everything but the past permissible.

Life is disorientating.
Perhaps he should meet her at the 'field of stelae'
where the murdered Jews of Europe
are somehow remembered in cement
for there is neither vantage point nor purchase.

Belief cannot survive in the open.
Before 'the turn', the world had meaning, electricity.

Sometimes he walks the streets at night when all the girls are gone.
He counts the city's paradoxes like blinding pairs of headlights.

Now the files are open, his flies are closed.
He is no longer 'Casanova'.
Time is a whore with her back to the wall—
and the wall is gone.

A PIECE OF CAKE
IN THE CAFÉ CENTRAL, VIENNA

Lost among the lunchtime Wieners, we debated how,
with the dreamy variety of cakes on display–
Punschkrapfen, Esterhazytorte, Apfelstrudel
Kardinalschnitte, Sachertorte und so weiter,
that cornucopia of chocolate, icing, and cream—
how the mechanics of their cake selection operate.
Having time on our hands we worked it out as follows:

A&B would browse the cabinets, select a cake,
inform the glowing fräulein who would pass them tickets
which, returning to their table they would give the waiter
when he finally found them among the drapes and columns,
who would slip them on his travels to the caketeer
in exchange for the appropriate confections, which
he would bring to A&B with a fruity 'viel Spaß!'

Finally we collared the slowest waiter—cousin
to their Peter Altenberg sitting life-like by the door–
and you declared we'd like *'Kaffee und kuchen. Bitte'.*
Hemmed in by other tables, we struggled to our feet,
eager for the ogling and selection to begin
when, half-turning to the cases thirty feet away,
he jerked his head and asked in inattentive English, 'Which?'

CLOUD WALKING AFTER AN ARGUMENT

'Soon clouds will blot out the fell,'
you announce grudgingly
as we climb from the village.

I fail to acknowledge it
but even St Mary's spire
is already lost in gauzy air.

Two soured sheep on Loughrigg,
we each savour the commonplace
intransigence of weather.

SCHMIDT'S 'ON SPECIAL' AT 67 CENTS

Drinking big, fruity California wines
and high-price microbrewery beers
at the Little America Hotel bar
in Flagstaff, Arizona. Chris and I
and you and your new girlfriend, Tuni,
shrugging shoulders over Brexit, Trump,
talking of where the two of you first met
and what our plans are for the morning,
how Oak Creek Canyon offers stellar views.
We talk of your hip and of my hearing

before slipping off into the small beer
of our student days. We've polished them,
the anecdotes, in random meetings
these past forty years. In my hands they tend
to ossify but Jim, in yours they take
their suppleness from incidental details
you remember, ones I've lost. Isn't it
always better sticking to the droll,
sidestepping the principles and passions
youth talks up—and time pisses away.

THE BACK COUNTRY, 1973

for Jim Todd

'To the faithful absence is condensed presence.'

One random Christmas night
in Williamsburg
with a new moon wasted
on the two of us

we slouched in the apartment
gone to cat grins,
the ashtray overwhelmed
with butts & roaches,
our souls poured out
with Distiller's Pride
& Pabst Blue Ribbon.

You were someone I was born with.

We dimmed Bob Dylan,
Astral Weeks, The Dead
to make exchanging gifts the thing—
my Dickinson & Browning
for your Snyder, Kesey.
The Back Country.

In a fit of mellow, opaque insight
Sometimes a Great Notion.
You hacked the cat's tail
of your blond braid off
& fixed it to the wall above your head.

We pondered it—
evolutionist and elegist —
until you wiped.
Then, high on symbolism,
I bundled you into my bed
my brother other self.

*

Tonight I unwind
and weave your braided hair,
dead friend.

BOHEMIA

'Paradise, like Bohemia, has no coast.'
– William Empson, 'Part of Mandevil's Travels'

Not for us the peace, prosperity and happiness,
the sylvan gardens of timeless contentment.
Better the gusty breath of the Vitava
shivering through the branches of autumnal lindens,
our words wind-snatched as we walk hand in hand,
a catch of cold air in our throats,
wending the river's course home to the sea.